The Gr: Possibilities

Inventor - Entrepreneur - Athlete

To Stas,

Love

Arlene Klein

An Inspirational Biography

The Grandfather of Possibilities

Second Edition

Published by Arlene Klein
P.O.Box 18747
Sarasota, Florida 34276-1747

www.designingpoet.com
www.thegrandfatherofpossibilities.com

Book design – Arlene and Ron Klein
Photographs – Copyright © 2008 by Ron Klein (First Edition)
Photographs – Copyright © 2014 by Ron Klein
ISBN-13:   978-0-9650915-4-1
ISBN-10:   0-9650915-4-6

To Ron, my loving husband, whose spirit and determination light the pages of this book. Life has been an incredible journey.

ALSO BY ARLENE KLEIN

I Never Wanted To Say Goodbye

CONTENTS

Acknowledgements

Authoring a book is a remarkably complex process. One starts with an amalgam of thoughts and ideas that eventually become the written word. With a reservoir of information, so graciously shared by family, friends and colleagues, this book became a reality.

My thanks to my mother-in-law and father-in-law for bringing Ron into the world and giving him the freedom to fly. My gratitude to Grandpa Samuel for everything you were and the legacy you left. You played a major role in the man Ron became. I wish I knew you, because I know I would have loved you.

To my son, Jeff, my love and appreciation for your enthusiasm and for introducing dad to Allan Horlick. If you hadn't planted the seed for me to think about writing this book, it may never have come to be. I'm ever so grateful for your invaluable input, which was so important to my writing. To my daughter, Lori, my love and thanks for the countless hours we spent talking on the telephone, making sure every detail was right. You encouraged me to tell a story worth telling. Thanks, Jeff and Lori, for reminders of many precious moments that I had long forgotten.

To my dear granddaughter, Erica, you are my sunshine. Little did you know, a third grade writing assignment would one day be published in a book. Your genuine words brilliantly shine herein.

Thanks to Allan Horlick for taking an interest in Ron's story and introducing Ron to Willie Jolley.

I sincerely want to thank Willie Jolley for believing in Ron. You'll never know how much your support, warmth and friendship means. Thanks to Dee Jolley for the perfect title for this book. To Robert McMillan, I want to say how much I appreciate your guiding hand. You, Willie, and Dee are a true inspiration.

I owe my gratitude to Linda Larsen, a good friend, who gave Ron countless hours of guidance. Thanks to my friends and fellow authors from Dog Writers' Association of America, who, so kindly, offered their help. Charlotte Reed, Liz Palika and Pat Santi, who took the time to listen to my questions and give me good answers. To my dear friend, Mordecai Siegal, who read the draft and so generously, offered suggestions and his professional opinion. Thanks for holding my hand and sharing your lifetime of literary experience.

I'll be forever grateful to my good friend, Patsy Wilson, who listened to me talk about a book in the making, read the draft and gave her honest opinion. To my respected friend, Pat Tway, thank you for your help and enthusiasm. To many friends and you know who you are, thank you for caring enough to read it.

Last, but not least, a kiss and hug to my beloved Yorkie, Scout, who was the loyal companion at my side as I toiled with every page. You taught me patience, the greatest lesson of all.

FOREWORD

Ron and his grandchildren are one heart. He was overwhelmed with joy, as Erica proudly handed him the paper. He placed it on his bookshelf, as a reminder of his granddaughter's love. As if he didn't already know it. In April 2001, Erica was nine years old. She was in the third grade in elementary school and was given an assignment to write a character sketch about someone she admired. A child's words hold true.

I have done my character sketch on my grandpa, Ron Klein. Some words to describe him are: energetic, kind, fun, athletic, artistic, smart, generous and very creative. He has invented things, very few can imagine. When my mom was young, he even made and sewed Halloween costumes for her. Each morning, my grandpa rides his bike 50 to 70 miles. He was also in the Senior Olympics and placed first in one of the bike races. He is kind in so many ways. I always enjoy visiting him. Whenever we go to my grandparents, he plays music with my sister, Mindy and me. He always encourages us to do our best. He is a lot of fun to be with, always smiling, pleasant and entertaining us with his jokes.

My grandpa is very smart. He is knowledgeable in many areas of business, science, computers and math. Generosity is a quality that he is also known for. He is very giving of his time and knowledge. Lastly, my grandpa is artistic. He is great at designing and drawing. When he was younger, he studied to be a commercial artist. However, he did not continue it as his career.

He loves animals, especially dogs. He and my grandma currently have 3 Yorkshire Terriers. His favorite wild animal is a tiger. My grandpa is a handsome man. He is about 5 feet 7 inches tall. His hair is brown and graying on the sides and his eyes are blue. He wears glasses.

I am very lucky to have him for a grandfather, because he is such a special person.

INTRODUCTION

How often do we meet someone who is a born survivor? Meet my husband, Ron Klein. From the time he was just a little boy, who built his own toys out of cardboard boxes, he has approached every challenge in life with a "can do" attitude. He wraps his arms around every problem and solves it. With logic, determination and ingenuity, he turns every negative into a positive.

He came into the world as a very ordinary kid and learned early on what the word challenge meant and how to deal with it. His growing up years were interrupted with illness and serious accidents. He always seemed to have the ability to bounce back.

His maternal grandfather, who was an inventor, had a great influence on him. As Ron became a teenager, his competence, creativity and talents surfaced. He was able to tackle anything with success. His independence, stamina and sensibility allowed him to use his skills at many jobs, to earn money that was so desperately needed.

When he turned eighteen years old, he was drafted into the Army during the Korean War. He served his country; experiencing all the hardships that one lives with in combat and was awarded a Purple Heart. His strength and compassion for others left him with many mixed emotions, but he landed on his feet and forged ahead.

Ron came into my life shortly after he returned to the states. He was everything I could have hoped for. He was smart, loving, caring and approachable. His soft-spoken, kind and humble manner was appealing.

He was a charming, good-looking man, with a wonderful sense of humor.

From the beginning days of his engineering career to his dynamic life on Wall Street, life has been an extraordinary journey. Every project was approached with a keen sense of clarity. His positive attitude and his integrity as a businessman and entrepreneur were the key ingredients for his success.

The challenges in business and in his personal life have always been met with the same "can do" attitude. His resilience never seems to falter.

Now he faces the biggest challenge. He is seventy-three years young and is living and coping with constant pain, caused by degenerative disc disease and spinal stenosis. Literally, that makes him physically challenged. Walking or standing for more than a few minutes cause more intense pain. But, once again, he figures out how to survive the adversity. He is an avid bicyclist and rides thirty miles a day, seven days a week. When he's on the bike, he's pain free and that's a reason to smile.
A positive attitude is my secret to success.

How we cope is all about attitude. Life has its ups and downs and we have to be able to roll with it. We all face challenges everyday and it's not always easy to hurdle the bumps in the road. Ron succeeds because he puts one foot in front of the other and keeps on going.

His story will touch the minds and hearts of those who come along on his journey. His experiences and his approach to solving problems will inspire anyone who has self-doubts. He is The Grandfather of Possibilities.

CHAPTER 1 the early years

It was 1935 and a year of uncertain times. Ron was born on July 6 in Philadelphia. His parents were honest, hard working people who had emigrated from Europe. His dad was a postal worker and his mom sold coats in a department store. Money was scarce; he and his older sister didn't have lavish toys, but Ron was content to amuse himself with simple crafts. He was a happy, curious child with a vivid imagination and his "can do" attitude was apparent early on. Using cardboard and masking tape, he became "Ronnie The Builder", creating a plethora of cars, airplanes and puppet theaters.

He was born with a love for fur and feathers. He loved all animals, no matter their size. At four years old he got his first dog, an Airedale Terrier who he named Happy. Years later, Spot, a Springer Spaniel, became another faithful companion. The dogs were his buddies and the pleasure he had when he was with them was undeniable. Nothing could keep them apart. He attempted to train his mom's two noisy, naughty parakeets. They were incorrigible! They chewed the wires on the dining room chandelier, ate an insurance policy and screamed whenever anyone was on the telephone. Ron flunked Bird Training 101.

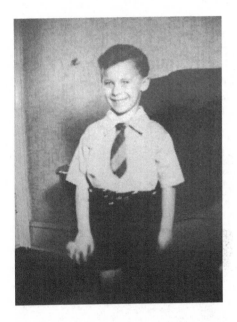

At a young age, he showed musical talents. A "virtuoso" at just six years old, he learned to play the guitar and banjo. His dad, who was musically inclined, taught him the basics. Together, they played and marched with the string bands in the Philadelphia Mummers Parade, until he was sixteen years old. During his high school years, he played guitar and bass in a small band with some of his friends, earning money playing at various affairs. As a contestant on the Paul Whiteman radio talent show, he won first prize playing the guitar. That win qualified him for the Paul Whiteman New York City television talent show, where he won first prize again.

Ron faced challenges early in his life. When he was four years old, he had Scarlet Fever. He remembers being carried out to the car to be taken to the hospital and seeing Happy at the door. He wasn't upset about being ill, but very distraught about having to leave his dog. At nine years old, he had a serious accident. He was walking across the street, where the telephone company was stringing wires for power lines. Just as he crossed, the wire caught him between the legs, lifting him in the air and dropping him to the ground. His head was split wide open and he had a concussion. He had another long hospital stay and many months to heal. At sixteen years old, he contracted Infectious Hepatitis. He was hospitalized and in isolation for three months. In those days, there was no such thing as modern medicine. He convalesced at home for a year. Since he couldn't be active, he kept himself busy by reading the Encyclopedia from cover to cover.

I was always curious and had a thirst for knowledge. Learning something new everyday would help me attain my goals for bigger and better things in life.

CHAPTER 2   a boy of many talents

Ron's grandfather had a great influence on how he developed. Ron idolized him and stuck to him like Velcro. Grandpa Samuel was a famous inventor, who invented the first Boiler Feeder for Tailors' Pressing Machines and the first set of television rabbit ears. In 1910, he was a joint inventor of the apparatus for the propulsion of ships. In June 1917, he invented the devices for protecting ships from torpedoes, submarines and mines. He was a diamond cutter, a magistrate and a great philosopher. Grandpa Samuel was a good tailor and he taught Ron how to use a sewing machine. Being a fast learner, he mastered the art of sewing and made his first guitar case out of canvas. When Grandpa Samuel died, Ron was with him and held him in his arms. He left Ron with wonderful memories of good times together and a treasure chest of wisdom and creativity.

Grandpa Samuel's cherished 1929 Model A Ford, named "Tony", was left to Ron. Being only sixteen years old and too young to appreciate the value of the car, he was more interested in having a new car. He sold the Model A Ford for one hundred dollars.
It was the mistake of my life.

Ron had artistic talents and was encouraged by his teachers to pursue a career in commercial art, so he went on to a vocational high school. He entered many poster contests and won first prize in the PSFS Bank contest in Philadelphia. After he graduated, he furthered his art studies at the Philadelphia Museum School of Art. He was also technically creative and excelled in building models and electrical, mechanical and technical devices.

With an affinity for horses, he taught himself how to ride English and Western saddle and rode five-gaited horses. Working at stables on weekends gave him the opportunity to bond with the animals he loved. He became a good rider and before long, was teaching horseback riding to young boys of the Police Athletic League.

He always needed money, so he tried his skills at many jobs while attending school. He worked in a candy factory, a wallpaper store and installed TV antennas on roofs. He even attempted to build a house with his cousin, who was a builder. He was fired from the job, when he dropped junk from the roof into an area, where the other workers kept their lunchboxes and thermos bottles.

I was never afraid to try something new and I always had a "can do" attitude.

CHAPTER 3   off to war

When he turned eighteen years old, he was drafted into the Army during the Korean War.

He served as an Artillery Fire Direction Control Specialist and Forward Observer. He was Private to PFC to Corporal to Staff Sergeant and demoted back to Corporal, when he sank a tank. His assignment was to escort six 155mm Howitzer tanks forward five miles. He was directed by his Captain to follow a dry riverbed five miles down, cross at the end of the riverbed and come five miles back on the other side and move forward. When he got to the riverbed, it didn't make sense for him to go ten additional miles, so he decided to cross the riverbed straight ahead. His personnel carrier tank was in the lead. When they got to the bottom of the riverbed, much to his surprise, they were in quicksand. The tank was gone in fifteen minutes. They all got out safely. He radioed back to headquarters, _"Send a truck to pick up my men. I lost my tank."_ Later, the US Army Corp of Engineers built a bridge, using the tank as a foundation.

I made a big mistake, but I learned a lesson. Sometimes, we have to listen to others who know more than we do.

He was discharged from the Army and returned home from Korea with a Purple Heart.

I wasn't a hero, just a man who served my country.

It was a tough time readjusting to civilian life. He had many mixed emotions, but his inner strength enabled him to overcome his feelings and move forward. However, to this day, his compassion for others never allows him to forget the horrific events of the war. There are some wounds that will never heal.

He was finally back to his normal self, when he had an almost fatal automobile accident. It was a head on collision that resulted in another hospital stay and more damage to his spine. The other driver was speeding, passed a red light at an intersection, swerved and hit him head on. Ron was flipped upside down in the car and his foot was caught in the steering wheel. The driver's door bolted open and Ron was dragged along the road on his head for more than a hundred yards. The car was totally demolished. It was a miracle that he survived. He was told that he might never walk again. With incredible resilience, he once again picked himself up and started all over again.

I was angry. My shiny Pontiac convertible was totaled. While I was in the Army, I saved all my money to buy the car. I was upset that I was a victim, but I was grateful to be alive and determined to move forward. I looked at the positive. I survived!

CHAPTER 4   staying afloat

In addition to having a commercial diploma, Ron took some classes and earned an academic diploma. He was so grateful for the GI Bill, which enabled him to enroll at Temple University.

Life was busy, to say the least, because he had to work while he was in college. He played guitar and bass in a small band to earn money and as the lead guitar player, he cut a record with a big band. He started a TV repair service. Work began at the end of the school day. He would make service calls to customers, come home and study into the wee hours of the morning. He did what he had to do, with no time to complain about too little sleep and barely any free time.

In 1958, Ron entered my life. A friend of mine, who played saxophone in the band, introduced us. Ron invited me out for our first date. He arrived, looking very collegiate in a pair of khaki pants and a light blue crew neck sweater. His winning smile and beautiful blue eyes attracted me, like bees to honey. We went to a little pizza parlor, where we talked and laughed for hours. When we drove back to my house, we sat in the car, listening to old favorites on the radio. He walked me to the door and kissed me good night. *Good night, skoshi. I'll call you tomorrow.* I think I knew then, that it would be the first of a lifetime of good night kisses. Not only was I crazy about him, but also, my parents loved him as much as I did.

After a few months of dating, we were engaged. We were in the car, heading out for a movie. Ron handed me a brown lunch bag, filled with boxes of candy. In the bag was a small, blue velvet box with my engagement ring. I was speechless! I should have realized that life would be full of surprises. Shortly after, I graduated with Certification in Medical Technology and Ron graduated college with a degree in Electrical Engineering. One year later, on September 27, 1959, we danced at our wedding. The Bass fiddle had to go. There was no room for the three of us in the car. We were happy and we were in love. I had visions of a lifetime with Ron, a couple of kids, dogs and a house. I had dreams of a quiescent life that we would live happily ever after. However, Ron had other ideas. We were one heart, but two minds.
I don't want an ordinary life. I want to be challenged. I want to accomplish things that can make a difference.

Little did I know what surprises were yet to come. I was in for the ride of my life. By the way, to this day, Ron still uses the Japanese and Korean word that means tiny or little. To him, I'm still *skoshi*.

On our honeymoon September, 1959

CHAPTER 5 new beginnings

Ron was trained in the new specialized field of digital computers and communications. His career in Electrical Engineering began as a technician with Honeywell Corporation, earning $97.00 a week. He was soon promoted to Computer Systems Design and Development Engineer, and developed a power control system for the Philadelphia Electric Company.

Not only was he advancing in his profession, but also, we soon became the proud parents of two children, our son Jeff, born in 1961 and our daughter Lori, born in 1963. Life was everything we hoped for. We were living the American dream. We had our first house, two children and two dogs, Trixie, a beautiful Smooth Collie and Tinkie, an adorable Yorkshire Terrier. Buttons, a precious mixed breed, joined our family a few years later.

The bills were mounting. So, Ron earned a few extra dollars selling frozen make at home pizzas, door to door.

I never thought that any job was beneath me. I did what I had to do and held my head high.

I was a busy stay at home Mom. Being a PTA participant, a Brownie Leader and a Cub Scout Den Mother kept me tightly entwined with Jeff and Lori's activities. Ron promised early on that he would be there for the children. He kept his promise and was, and has always been present in their lives. He made time to be a Boy Scout Cub Master and Little League umpire during Jeff's growing up years. We sat through ten years of dance recitals and years of tennis matches and enjoyed every minute. We were sponges, absorbing the pleasure of our children's accomplishments. We loved being parents and embraced our time together as a family.

I was always dedicated to my wife and children. They're my life.

CHAPTER 6 super man on the move

In 1964, Ron left Honeywell, taking a position as Director of Engineering with Ultronics Systems Corp., which later was acquired by GT&E Financial Data Services. He was flying all over the country and averaging a half a million miles a year. He was employed by GT&E until 1968, during which time he invented the magnetic strip credit card and the Validity Checking System. This invention was awarded a United States Patent. The patent is Validity Checking System. The patent can be viewed at www.Google.com/patents Insert number 3465289.

I recognized that I had an opportunity. Having the self-confidence to meet the challenge and knowing my strengths, I moved forward with a positive, "can do" attitude.

GT&E had a large client, who was in the retail business. Every month, the credit card companies gave all retailers a list of poor credit risks, which was comprised of thousands of credit card account numbers. When a customer came to pay for their purchase, the salesperson had to go through the list, to see if the customer's credit card number appeared. The process was very time consuming, especially at holiday time.

Ron felt that the problem could be solved with a simple process. He would store all of the credit risk account numbers in a memory device and place a keypad, where the salesperson could key in the account number. If the memory device did not flag the customer's account number, the account was fine. To speed up the process, he felt that *"smarts"* could be placed into the plastic credit card. He tried placing coded holes in the card, which would represent the credit card account number.

Then, he discovered a better idea. Tape recorders were relatively new at that time. If he would paste a piece of magnetic tape on the back of the card and record the account number onto the tape, it could be placed into a small tape reader and be sent to the memory device to be read. It worked fine, so he went to a company that manufactured plastic credit cards and asked if they could impregnate a magnetic material on the back of the credit cards. They said it was possible. Thus, came the Validity Checking System that is used for checking the validity of credit cards.

Every problem can be solved, by reducing it to a simple, logical form that is understandable.

In 1968, he moved on to explore his entrepreneurial spirit and founded his new company, Technitrend, Inc. A technician, who worked for him at GT&E, joined him and became his partner. He was a genius, with extraordinary design talents. It was a perfect partnership and a great friendship. Ron was the businessman, who created and developed the ideas. His partner was the engineer, who brought the ideas to fruition. Their first project involved developing a system for a nutrition company, which enabled the growth of healthier chickens in eight weeks, which was less than the usual long-term growth period. That was the beginning of the company's involvement in the design and manufacture of data communications systems and products.

During the early years of Technitrend's growth, Ron developed two computer systems. One is used in the banking industry to provide computerized voice response. The second is used in the real estate industry to provide computerized multiple listing services.

The mental anguish of cash flow problems was haunting. With every turn, there were bills to pay and a weekly payroll to meet. The problems grew worse everyday. Where was the money going to come from? How would Ron meet the challenge?

I believed in myself and worrying was a waste. When confronted with the problems, I thought logically and took action.

He registered Technitrend, Inc. with the Securities and Exchange Commission for a public stock offering. Those were the days that any company with a technical name had a successful stock offering. *It was hell on earth!* Simultaneous to running the company on a daily basis, he had to deal with the demands of the Wall Street gurus. *What an education it was. It took a lot to stay calm and focused, while all was going on.* Finally, after many months, the offering was successfully completed. The funding enabled the company's continued growth. Technitrend became a large company, employing technical and manufacturing staff. They soon outgrew the two small buildings they were leasing. Ron designed and had built, from the ground up, the company's engineering and manufacturing plant.

There were one hundred twenty-five employees to pay each week. The problems became insurmountable.

The manufacturing staff threatened to unionize. Everyone was being paid better than union wages, so there was not a legitimate reason to unionize. Ron went into the manufacturing area, climbed onto the highest workbench. *This is your company and I have no idea why you want to destroy it. So, I've made the decision to immediately shut the company down. You're all out of work. However, at two o'clock this afternoon, Human Resources will be taking applications for my new company that will be starting immediately. This will be an excellent opportunity for those of you who don't want to unionize, to apply.* Immediately after he spoke, everyone cheered, "Let's keep the company the way it is now."
We never had a union threat again.
I solved a major problem with strength and a smile on my face.

It was January 1970, when we got a phone call. His partner was killed in an automobile accident, while driving down an icy road. He lost control, hit a tree and died instantly. It was a few days before his twenty-ninth birthday. He left a wife and two small children. Ron and I were devastated.
I had to deal with the tragedy and keep everything glued together. It wasn't easy.

Ron held the majority shares of Technitrend stock until late 1970, at which time he sold his interest to a major insurance company. He continued as Chief Executive Officer, until his resignation in 1972.

His partner was gone. The company was no longer a part of our life. It was under the control of the insurance company and its subsidiary.

Our beautiful tapestry had unraveled. However, many of the pressures of running a large company, dealing with the people and answering to the Wall Street market makers was over.

I wanted to change direction and control my own destiny.

With tireless spirit, he was about to start his next enterprise, but was moving onward in uncharted waters. He knew that he wanted something that would not be labor intensified, but would guarantee repeated revenue. There was no strategic plan, but he was concentrating his efforts on data communications.

Needing income in the beginning stages of a new venture, he took the Real Estate exam and became involved with a homestead development project in Florida. It was very successful.

I challenged my mind, learned a lot and accomplished my goals in a brand new area. He also was putting food on the table.

In April 1972, he founded General Associates, Inc. Once again, he wanted to be his own person and experience the challenge of growth. He started by representing other companies' products in the field of data communications. During a sales visit to a large client, he noticed a bid offering from the Western Union Telegraph Company on the client's desk. He asked the client about the offering and was told that they had no interest and he was welcome to the bid offering.

Western Union was the major provider of TWX and TELEX teleprinters, which were used in the early days of communications, to provide printed messages to and from users over communication lines. In those days, they were also used as input/output terminals for personal computers, before the development of video terminals.

He won the bid, brought the machines home, cleaned them in the basement with mineral spirits, and stored them in the garage. The smell of the spirits permeated the house, as it came through the heat vents. One day a customer came to our house to buy a teleprinter. He asked, "Miss, could I use your men's room?" I sent him to the powder room in our house. He didn't have good aim and that was the day that I directed Ron "out of the house" with all the machines and equipment. To this day, he still tells everyone what a favor I did for him. He rented space in a building and became a real company. However, he was a one-man company, except for the days when I would take the dogs and go to the office to do his clerical work. Shortly after, he hired a helper to refurbish the few teleprinters he had won on the original bid.

As a special service, he refurbished special teleprinters for the hearing impaired. The teleprinters were used with acoustic telephone couplers, so that hearing impaired people could communicate with the hearing. He modified special teleprinters that would impregnate paper tape with the Braille code, so that the visually impaired could read typed messages received over communication lines.

In 1975, Western Union placed all of the teleprinter inventory up for bid. Western Union was moving in a new direction of business, utilizing satellite services. General Associates was the successful bidder and acquired twelve thousand teleprinters for pennies on the dollar. Now, he had a business! He was in the used and refurbished TWX and TELEX teleprinters business and became the distributor of teleprinters and parts, to leading global communications companies throughout the U.S.

Four thousand units were stored within travel distance of the General Associates location. The other eight thousand units were located at various major hubs throughout the country. The majority of these units were large and weighed hundreds of pounds. Shipping was out of the question. He had a major problem and he had to solve it. He was in a vulnerable position and had to do something fast. How was he going to deal with this? He handled it as he handled all other challenges in his life. The "can do" attitude surfaced. He couldn't afford to take possession and move eight thousand machines, so he had to be very inventive. Most of these machines were manufactured in the early 1950's and had electronic printed circuit cards in the control sections, which contained gold traces. Gold was used in those days, because it provided best conductivity and was very inexpensive. He collaborated with a foreign government to scrap and process thousands of the circuit cards and share the profits of the gold meltdown. He was very fortunate that year, because gold had multiplied twenty times in value. He now owned all of the machines at no cost. However, he still had thousands of pounds of scrap metal that had to be disposed of.

With careful investigation, he discovered that the metal teleprinter cabinets contained large amounts of chromium. At that time, a foreign car manufacturer needed chromium for its automobile bodies. What a great way to dispose of the thousands of pounds of scrap metal. They took care of the overseas shipping. Ron had the balance of four thousand very valuable teleprinters that he could refurbish and sell to his clients. What could have been a complete catastrophe became a very profitable venture.

This was a real challenge. I was innovative and turned a negative into a positive.

He hired two more people to refurbish the machines and sort the parts. Ron got his hands dirty, working with his employees. Then, he would put on a jacket and a tie and be the salesman. I continued to work at the office three days a week.

Again, the cash flow problem showed its ugly head. There were bills mounting and people to pay. But, we bit the bullet, borrowed money to meet the obligations and Ron forged ahead.

He was like a bowling ball rolling down the alley. There was no stopping now. The more involved he became, the more confidence he had with his new enterprise. He was on a mission and I knew he would attain his goals. Well, I hoped and prayed!

I was confident that I would achieve my goals. I was prepared to change direction, if I had to.

In 1979, the New York Stock Exchange contacted Western Union, requesting special teletypewriter equipment that they needed to support their requirements for trading floor expansion. Western Union referred NYSE to General Associates. General Associates sold the equipment to NYSE and established operations at the New York Stock Exchange, providing maintenance and service for trading floor operations. It gave General Associates an excellent opportunity to offer the NYSE technical expertise in the area of hardware and software development. The NYSE gave General Associates office space at the Stock Exchange at 11 Wall Street.

Other things were happening in 1979. There was a fuel crisis. There was a limited amount of fuel available and long lines at the gas pumps. It was difficult for people to travel long distances. Ron had an automobile that required diesel fuel. Diesel, a by-product of gasoline, was also limited in supply. However, there was no limitation on the delivery of home heating fuel.

Ron learned that number two home heating oil was the same as diesel fuel, except for one difference. In very cold weather, home heating fuel would coagulate and become very thick. However, there was a product on the market that could correct the coagulation problem. Just a very small amount of the product had to be added to the home heating fuel. So, he purchased a two hundred seventy-five gallon home heating fuel tank and put it in the garage. He elevated it on six-foot stilts, so that it could provide gravity feed, and he built a hose with a gas station type nozzle. His fuel crisis was solved!

He was guaranteed to have fuel in his tank for the two hundred mile commute back and forth to New York everyday. Better yet, home heating fuel was cheaper than diesel fuel at the gas station.

The maintenance service that General Associates provided required exchanging faulty teleprinters on the trading floor with spare units. Ron would take the faulty units back to the plant in New Jersey and return with repaired units the next morning. It was difficult to carry the repaired units back to the NYSE from the Battery Park Garage, where he parked his car. So, he bought a USPS Mail Jeep and had one of his employees pick him up at the parking lot with the jeep and drive him to the NYSE at 11 Wall Street. They would pull up to the front door, in between all of the limousines that arrived with the NYSE executives. It was quite a sight, but it worked for him.

I was never concerned or bothered by what anyone had to say about it. How good is that?

General Associates' speed, proficiency and technical expertise in the field of financial data systems and services earned Ron great credibility with the New York Stock Exchange and the financial community. Their capabilities resulted in the ongoing development of special products and services to support financial trading. As General Associates became more involved with high priority projects, the NYSE provided General Associates additional space on the stock exchange trading floor to support operations.

Someone once told me that I was lucky. I disagreed. Yes, maybe I was lucky to be at the right place at the right time. But, if I didn't recognize opportunity and take advantage of it, I wouldn't be so lucky.

Life was exciting, but with the fame and glory came a myriad of headaches and problems. Ron approached every situation with his typical "can do" attitude.

CHAPTER 7   life goes to the dogs

Life on the home front was business as usual. We always tried to maintain a normal existence, in spite of Ron's crazy schedules and paramount problems. Jeff and Lori were never aware of the anxieties we faced. They were not affected and rolled merrily along. There were days when my nerves were frayed and I just wanted to scream, "Enough." The children became teenagers, went off to college and were well on their way to building their careers.

Now, it was time to begin my own personal journey. Ron became my driving force. Not only was he the role model that inspired me to do my own thing, but he gave me the confidence to believe in myself and discover my own talents.

We're all capable of moving in any direction we want. If you have a passion for what you do, anything is possible.

A few weeks after Lori left for college, Ron and I attended our first dog show. We had the time of our life, took pictures of every dog and never stopped smiling. We were like two kids in a toy store. With my passion for dogs, I thought showing dogs would be perfect for me. Now, I was on a mission. I made up my mind that I wanted to get a beautiful Yorkshire Terrier and become involved in Breed Conformation. Ron thought it was a great idea and supported me all the way. I was starting a new chapter in the world of dogs.

In February 1982, we traveled to New York, attended Yorkshire Terrier Specialty shows and the Westminster Kennel Club Dog Show at Madison Square Garden. After many months of studying pedigrees and gathering information, I selected a breeder and got my first precious puppy. Talk about a challenge; he was a handful. He taught me everything I had to know. Ron and I became addicted to "the dog game." Oh, the places we went and the people we met, thanks to an adorable five pound yappy Yorkie.

Before long, our canine family grew and we were sharing our home with six Yorkshire Terriers. They all became show dogs, but they were our pampered babies. Ron was like a mother hen. He couldn't get enough of them. We were living "middle age crazy!" I loved the dogs with all my heart. I learned so much from them; from living with them, observing them and interacting with them. Being in the ring with them was the icing on the cake and I was proud of the American Champions that I owner handled and finished.

It was an era filled with magical moments and I just wanted time to stand still.

But, it was quickly passing by. Our children graduated college and Jeff graduated Law School. They married and started their families. Soon, we were the proud grandparents of four beautiful grandchildren. Our love and devotion to animals was passed on to them. They adored the dogs and now have pets of their own.

After a long day of the helter-skelter pace on Wall Street, Ron took the two-hour drive home to New Jersey. He shed his suit and tie, put on a pair of khakis and a sweatshirt and sat on the floor, surrounded by six bundles of fur. I smiled, as I saw the pressures of his day melt away. The dogs grabbed his heart and never let go. When weather permitted, we put all of the dogs in the car and drove to the center of town. With leashes in hand, we walked down Main Street with six perfectly groomed, well-mannered Yorkies. Pedestrians and shopkeepers would stop to see "our precious pooches on parade."

Ron continues to play an important part in my world and he savors every minute. As my videographer, Webmaster, illustrator and technical guru, we are a team. Best of all, we've shared a lifetime together with lots of fur at our feet.

The happiness and unconditional love the dogs gave was a story I wanted to share with the world. I wanted to pay tribute to my dogs and make a difference for all companion animals.

My passion for animal health and welfare was first and foremost. I produced a video on responsible pet ownership, and authored and published a booklet of poems on pet loss. Both were nominated for Dog Writers' Association of America Awards. One of my poems was selected and published in a book, written by an award-winning author. There were articles for national publications, invitations to speak on pet loss, and interviews for magazines and radio talk shows. I became a member of DWAA and was invited to judge writing competition, and I became affiliated with many animal related organizations. The dogs and I were filmed for a DWAA award winning video.

For the past seventeen years, I have worked with the Morris Animal Foundation, a national animal health foundation that funds studies worldwide for prevention, treatment and cure for diseases that affect all species of animals that share our world.

Ron and I have lost nine dogs. When it was time to say good–bye to them, we held on tight to each other and cried. Each dog had a special place in our life and each holds a special place in our hearts.

Now, we have just one Yorkshire Terrier. He's gorgeous, smart and very special. Scout is ten years old and has been an American Champion, since he was two years old. He's the essence of joy! He's our constant companion and our best company, as he joins us everywhere in "pet friendly" Sarasota. I still show him occasionally and it's another magical moment as he prances around the ring. Proud Ron is always at ringside taking pictures and cheering us on.

CHAPTER 8 the dog castle

I never knew what Ron was up to. He was full of surprises.

We were so happy in the lovely house in Cherry Hill, New Jersey. If walls could talk, they would tell the fairy tale story about nineteen wonderful years of memorable times. We raised our children in that house. There was the tree house that Ron built for them. There were memories hiding in every corner. Yes, there were many sad times. We lost our parents and many loved ones and the house was busy with people coming to pay their respects. But, for the most part, the house was alive with parties and dinners to celebrate holidays and special occasions. We shared happy moments with friends, family and business associates. It was also getting crowded with six dogs.

CHAPTER 8 *the dog castle*

In July 1987, I casually said to Ron, "I would love to have a larger house, with more space and less wooded grounds, for the dogs." Later that week, our painter of many years stopped in to say hello. I repeated to him what I had said to Ron about a larger house. He told me that he had just finished painting a brand new house in Moorestown and that it was for sale. The owner had hired an architect to design the house. Just weeks before he and his wife were to move in, she suddenly died.

I called the realtor and Ron and I took a ride to see the house. "Oh my!" It was something out of a magazine. It was six thousand square feet and had beautiful grounds. It was exactly what I wanted, but it was out of the question and definitely out of our price range. We talked about it and I dreamt about it, but we shelved the idea.

A few days later, I left on a trip to England to attend dog shows in Windsor. I called Ron on July 6 to wish him a happy birthday. *Honey, I made an offer on the house.* I was dumbfounded. When I returned home the following week, I had barely unpacked my suitcase, when the phone rang. His offer on the house was accepted. I was in a panic. Ron said that if I didn't want to move, he was still going to buy the house and resell it.

Six weeks later, we closed on the house, made the additions and changes that would accommodate our precious puppies and moved to our castle. The rooms were so large that the great room became both a living room and a dining room. The original dining room was converted to the "dog room." We had the floor tiled and the room decorated with a border of Ralph Lauren wallpaper with a dog motif. An entire wall was glass from floor to ceiling. It was perfect for the dogs to lull in their beanbag pillows and watch everyone go by. One corner of the room was where I groomed the dogs. In a cove was a plastic fireplug. It couldn't get any better. The carpenter built solid oak gates, for the dogs' safety. It was the talk of the town. Of course, the dogs were never confined to the room. It was where they stayed if we weren't home or if they just wanted to retreat to their own place. Otherwise, they had freedom throughout the house and they loved to run up the long hallways to be with us in the bedroom at night. We also had the carpenter replace a window in the laundry room with a door that led out to a huge deck, that he built for the dogs to exercise and bask in the sun. Our treasured Yorkies lived happily ever after in the lap of luxury.

I loved those dogs and their comfort was important to me. There wasn't anything I wouldn't do for them.

When Ron and I would travel for business or pleasure, the dogs' comforts were never compromised. Ron's secretary, who bred Yorkies and had five of her own dogs, would move into the house. Now, there were eleven "barking bedroom slippers" running and playing in the dog room in the castle.

Ron made it all happen so smoothly. He handled the complications of selling the Cherry Hill house and the move to the castle with the typical "can do" attitude. I was knee deep in work: deciding what to keep and what to let go, sorting out and packing up from the house that held all our memories and moving to the castle, with six curious Yorkies at my side.

The castle was alive with people and parties, as was the house in Cherry Hill. We had nine glorious years there, until we made our permanent move to Sarasota.

CHAPTER 9 bigger and better

In 1983, Ron developed a system to provide up to the minute bond quotation and trade information for the members of the New York Stock Exchange and other financial institutions. He successfully negotiated a contract with the New York Stock Exchange, to become a licensed financial vendor to disseminate quotes and trades of New York Stock Exchange listed bonds.

The project started when he saw that the New York Stock Exchange traded bonds on a bond-trading floor. When the bond traders in the Wall Street offices wanted to know the prices, they had to call in by telephone to their contact on the New York Stock Exchange bond-trading floor. Ron thought this was very antiquated. There was automated quotation service for stocks. Why not for bonds?

So, he developed a prototype system that would enable the pricing of bonds from the bond-trading floor, to appear at the bond broker's desk at their Wall Street office. How would he market it? The traders were always extremely busy and it was impossible to talk to them during trading hours. He did not have the resources to advertise in the Wall Street Journal or other expensive media. So, he gave the system to a bond manager that he befriended, who was with a leading Wall Street firm. That manager did extremely well, by having the prices before anyone else, and he topped the other brokers' bids. It wasn't too long before the other firms were asking, "How are you able to top our bids so quickly?" He answered, "You need General Associates' Bond Quote Monitor." The phones started to ring off the hook with orders. Ron couldn't get the monitors installed fast enough. Fifty percent of all the firms on Wall Street became customers. The project was very successful. It provided transparency and was operational for more than a quarter of a century.

I made something happen, by knowing how to recognize opportunity and using ingenuity.

As the New York Stock Exchange functions grew, the space that General Associates occupied had to be used for trading floor expansion. General Associates was moved to the New York Stock Exchange sub-basement, next to the men's locker room. There were many funny stories of the days in the basement.

In 1985, he developed a video display system to support trading of US Government bonds, bills, notes and government agency products. All primary financial institutions that trade Government issues through inter-market financial brokers presently use these systems.

In the years to follow, General Associates provided the video display systems and a variety of other products to the American Stock Exchange, Philadelphia Stock Exchange, New York Futures Exchange and New York Comex Exchange.

General Associates was not IBM. They were just a small company. However, they met the needs, saved the Exchanges a lot of money and always got the job done. Ron was a man of his word.

Whatever I promised, I delivered.

His accomplishments were paramount. It was an exciting and dynamic time, but there were always problems that arose and had to be solved.

I met the challenge with a keen sense of clarity and a positive attitude.

CHAPTER 10   time to play

Ron's hands and mind were never idle. He was always fixing, designing or building something. Of course, I had no complaints. He was better than any handy man that I could have hired. Every job, no matter how big or small, was done to perfection. He would approach every task methodically and meticulously. If it was something that he didn't know as much about as he thought he should, he researched it and then proceeded to complete the task. He loved the challenge and never said, *I can't do it.*

When he had free time, he read Gray's Anatomy. It wouldn't be the average man's choice of reading, but of course, Ron is not the average man.

He was always doing something creative with the children. There were the Halloween costumes he made, the model of our cabin cruiser he built from balsa wood, all the science projects they did together and the pinewood derby cars that he and Jeff designed and built.

And heaven forbid, the children ask him, "Dad, what keeps an airplane in the sky?" The poor kids would have to sit and listen to an hour explanation. But, to this day, I'm sure they know what keeps an airplane in the sky. There was very little that Ron didn't know about. If he didn't, he was absolutely going to learn about it to the nth degree.

There were the projects he did, just because he felt like doing them. He built a television out of scrap parts and a wood console to house it.   There was the buggy that he and a friend built, that adorned our driveway for months. It was a replica of the first automobile and was built with a tiller and bicycle wheels and was painted black. He built two player pianos. One was painted red and was donated to a children's home. The other was painted black and was a gift to our granddaughters. What next?

When the new high technology devices were developed and were stocked on store shelves, Ron was in his glory. He was a man before his time and understood each and every computer, telephone, camera and other electronic gadget inside and out. Knowing how everything worked, he could trouble shoot any problem that arose. The phone rang constantly with calls from friends, who just couldn't figure out how to operate everything. It was future shock for most of us.

Ron always loved music and he never gave up playing his guitar. I was thoroughly convinced that if he had set his mind to it, he could have been a Country music star. But, he just enjoys strumming. The children and I share his enthusiasm and our grandchildren think he's "cool." When they come to our house, everyone will grab percussion instruments that we brought back from the islands and we have a jam session. Sometimes, Ron will play the guitar and I'll play the piano and we'll just have fun. He also bought a djembe drum and goes to the drum circle at the beach with the young, the old, the rich and the poor to "beat the drum and feel the beat."

Throughout his working years, he always had fun with his "grown up" toys. He loved foreign cars and acquired old vintage models and refurbished them. He loved getting his hands dirty. He would have the cars towed home and then he started the project. He would fix the engines, burn the paint off and then paint them with primer. They were ready to be finished. Then he sold them. It was a short-lived interest that lasted only a few months. I thanked my lucky stars, because we were running out of space in the driveway.

He was always interested in boating. In the mid 1960's, he bought our first boat, a little runabout. We loved family outings on the river. It wasn't too long, before he bought a cabin cruiser.

We were taking family weekend trips in the bay and ocean along the New Jersey shore. After a few years of motorboats, he yearned to sail and bought a twenty-foot day sailor.

A few years later, he graduated to a thirty-foot sailboat for ocean racing and cruising. That was the last of the boats, until he bought a kayak, when we moved to Florida.

That's our summerhouse in the background

Having the love of the water and seashore life, he decided to use his artistic talents and architectural skills, to design and build a summerhouse for us. We enjoyed our good times together as a family, but we wanted a house on the water. We purchased a waterfront lot and Ron set his talents to work again, designing a more beautiful house. We spent the first summer there and it seemed perfect, but it wasn't exactly right for the dogs. So, once again we were in the building mode. Ron designed what he wanted and the builder put an addition on the house. Now, our canine family had the same comforts as they had in the castle in Moorestown.

For his fiftieth birthday, I planned a party at our new summerhouse. I invited a lot of family and friends. The house was nice size and had three large decks. It was seven thirty in the morning, the day of the party, and Ron thought it would be a good idea to have the builder enlarge one of the decks. So, they brought out the crane and pile drivers and started to build. The heat that day was an intense ninety-four degrees. The caterers were in the kitchen, preparing for the guests. Our six Yorkies were running through the house. It was sheer chaos. The builder was finished at five thirty in the evening and the guests started to arrive at six o'clock.

The party was a huge success. The construction completion was a close call and it was a crazy thing to do. But, that's Ron! We enjoyed eleven wonderful summers there, until we became full time residents in Sarasota.

He had such a great time building houses that he decided to buy five more waterfront lots, and design and build five more houses to sell. He discovered that the lots were subject to the wetlands act and that in one year there would be a moratorium on building on those specific lots.

He offered the owner of the lots a buy-out on all five pieces at a discounted price and she accepted. Conventional construction would have been impossible to complete in one year. He researched the manufacturers of pre-fabricated houses and discovered that there were attractive, inexpensive houses that could be purchased and delivered to the home site and erected in thirty days. In less than a year, he successfully sold the lots with the houses and beat the moratorium.

I carefully analyzed what I was about to do and made sure there was a safe way out. I approached the challenge with self-confidence and my "can do" attitude.

CHAPTER 11 the greatest gift of all

Ron's retired now, but still holds the position as Chairman of General Associates. After two years as snowbirds in Sarasota, Florida in a condo that we purchased in 1994, we became permanent residents in 1996. We sold our three properties and purchased a lovely villa.

Our daughter and son-in-law and two granddaughters live in Orlando and our son and daughter-in-law and two grandsons live in Boca Raton. We live in a tropical Paradise and have our family within driving distance. How lucky we are!

Life has changed. It always does. It becomes a time to think about what's really important.

Philanthropic involvement has always been a big part of our life. We've always volunteered our services for worthwhile causes and feel well rewarded for our commitment to something bigger than ourselves.

From the very beginning of his business days, Ron would get calls from our friends' children and our children's friends, asking for career advice.

How well I remember the hours he spent mentoring so many young people, who are now well established in their careers and professions. Many of them worked for him during summer break, learning from the ground up about business and entrepreneurship. They were starry-eyed, when they spent time at the New York Stock Exchange, learning about the financial marketplace. How lucky our children were to have Ron as their Dad. They had him in their hip pocket and benefited from the wisdom and experience he shared with them.

In 1993, he taught Entrepreneurship, pro bono, as an adjunct professor at Temple University, School of Business and Management.

Ron Klein, chairman of General Associates, Inc., demonstrates electronic trading to finance majors.

When we moved to Sarasota, he volunteered his services for six years with the Sarasota County Sheriff's Office, assisting deputies with community policing.

Whether planning Bike-A-Thons as fundraisers for my non-profits, developing the first database system for non-profits, serving on steering committees or advisory boards or just helping a little old lady find her car on the parking lot, it's been a rewarding experience for him.

Early in August 2008, we were at the beach, enjoying the privilege of another day in paradise. It was not an ordinary day, because the usually calm Gulf of Mexico was a sea of roaring surf. Storms of previous days had left their mark. Ron and I sat in silence. I was deep in thought about the hurricanes of past years and the toll they had taken on people. We're living in troubled times; devastating natural disasters, terrorist threats, a falling economy and a slumping housing market. Ron must have been reading my mind. The silence was broken.

I'm going to do inspirational speaking.

"What?"

People are hurting. Their hopes and dreams are shattered. Their confidence is broken. If I can help just one person solve some of their problems, I'll be satisfied.

"What drives you?"

Need!

"Need?"

Yes, need to change things, need to make something better, need to make a difference.

"When will you stop?"

When I'm dead! You know, if you stand still, they throw dirt on you. If you're not busy living, you're busy dying.

"But, you never relax."

I'm always relaxed. If I'm doing what I love to do, I'm relaxed. If I'm doing something that I don't want to do, I'm not happy. Besides, Scout is the best therapist. I look in his eyes and I see his soul. I think I'm going to get my story together and make a few calls to get speaking engagements.

The man I have been married to for forty-nine years, the man I know inside and out, just invited me into his innermost thoughts. His aspirations and goals will never stop.

CHAPTER 12 the biggest challenge

Ron is seventy-three years old and is living everyday with constant pain. He has degenerative disc disease and spinal stenosis and he's trying to cope with it.

Literally, he's physically challenged. Walking or standing for more than a few minutes exacerbates the problem and causes more intense pain. His condition has been determined by numerous neurosurgeons to be inoperable. He has had many serious accidents that have aggravated his back problems. He has had treatment and physical therapy. Nothing has given him relief. Since his condition was diagnosed in 2004, it has progressed. *I don't want to take pain medication, because I want to keep my mind alert.*

The last serious accident was in 2001, while training for a bicycling competition. He remembered turning his head to look at the beach. *The water is so blue today.* He remembered nothing after that, until he opened his eyes in the hospital emergency room. It was early afternoon and I got the call from his friend, who was riding with him that day. "Arlene, Ron's had an accident.

We were drafting and he clipped the bike in front of him and went down. He's unconscious and badly bruised. The paramedics are taking him to Sarasota Memorial. I'll meet you there." My heart was thumping in my chest. I jumped in my car and got to the hospital. I entered the emergency room and waited and waited and waited, but Ron never arrived with the paramedics. My heart was sinking. Was he dead? After an hour of waiting, the nurse came over to me, "Mrs. Klein, there was an accident on Ringling Bridge and the paramedics couldn't cross the bridge to get here. They had to take Mr. Klein to Blake Medical Center in Bradenton." I got into the car and drove to Blake, almost an hour of driving in heavy traffic. I entered a crowded emergency room and found Ron on a stretcher; his entire left side from head to toe was covered with road rash. He recognized me, but he was making no sense. I tried to decipher what he was saying, but couldn't understand a word. The nurse wheeled him to another room for x-rays and tests. I waited and tried to keep my composure. When he was wheeled back, he was still covered with the road dirt and I started to clean him up a little. The emergency room staff was on overload, with sick and injured people. I did my best to make him comfortable and I left the hospital at midnight and drove home. I was weary and worried. They discharged him the next day and I picked him up. He was smiling and he sounded crazy. He had a mild concussion and temporary amnesia. In the days that followed, we were running to doctors for more tests to determine why he had blacked out. Ron and I were both exhausted. By some miracle, he escaped the accident with no serious injuries. He had only cuts and bruises. His memory returned in a few weeks. Six weeks later, he was back on his bike and ready to ride.

Ron is an avid bicyclist! He rides thirty miles a day, seven days a week. He began riding for pleasure and fitness more than twelve years ago and has logged more than one hundred thirty thousand miles. In 1999, he became a competitive bicyclist. He earned gold medals in the Siesta Key Triathlons. He was a medal winner in the Sarasota County Senior Olympics and the Florida State Championship Senior Olympics. In 2003, he was Athlete of the Year in Sarasota County. The children and I were thrilled to watch him compete and we were so proud to see him carry the torch. Never did he dream that a hobby and fitness program would become his salvation. He's one hundred percent pain free when he rides his bike in the racing position. The multiple pinched nerves in his spine are released and he has instant relief. The doctors have told him that because of his fitness, his legs and abdominal muscles are so strong that he is able to function and not be confined to a wheelchair. Needless to say, he loves the joy of riding. The relief he gets each day helps him cope.

It is euphoria for me and keeps me smiling

CHAPTER 13 staying upright

Ron was mentally prepared to meet the challenges of growing older. However, he didn't expect his golden years to bring him more than just aches and pains. But, life is good. We are alive; we have a great marriage of forty-nine years, wonderful children, terrific grandchildren and a little Yorkshire Terrier at our side. It's all a reason to get up every morning and smile.

Life has been a roller coaster ride, but Ron's business like strategy has overcome my emotionality. Throughout our forty-nine years, Ron never lost sight of the most important thing to him; his love and devotion to me, the children, grandchildren and the precious dogs. He's happy and content, with wonderful memories of his past accomplishments. He is responsible for taking us from our humble beginning to where we are now. It's been an incredible journey. Together, we've traveled a long and winding road, embracing every step along the way. We have overcome the obstacles and have celebrated our victories.

He never had to struggle to find his place. His place is wherever he is and whatever he's doing. He's comfortable with himself and with others.

He doesn't have to raise the bar. He's done it all. Yet, he keeps challenging his mind to learn something new everyday. He continues to achieve and accomplish whatever he sets out to do, with a smile on his face and a twinkle in his eye. He has a lust for life and lives every moment to the fullest.

Life now is far less complicated and we love it. Our possessions are fewer and so are the headaches of bygone days. We share the memories of magical moments. Actually, our life is richer now, because we have all the time in the world to spend with each other. We're not plagued with the myriad of problems that could have pulled us apart.

However, I'm smart enough to know that Ron is on another mission and will succeed with his new venture. As he talks about his plans to do inspirational speaking, he reminds me of the enthusiastic young man that I met more than a half century ago.

As we walk along Main Street, hand in hand, Ron walks at a slower pace than he did on Wall Street. But, that's okay. He's still upright and determined to keep himself upright for as long as he can. *Skoshi, I'll take my ride tomorrow at eight thirty. I should be back by eleven o'clock.* He's a free spirit, riding into the wind on his bike and he plans to keep riding until the bitter end. He's invincible. He's The Grandfather of Possibilities.

RON KLEIN'S LESSONS FOR LIFE

Be dedicated to your family. They are your life.

Believe in yourself.

Your security is your own self -confidence.

Always have a "can do" attitude.

Be a good listener. We learn something new everyday.

Whatever adversities life has in store for you, try to deal with it. I know, as you do, it's not always easy.

Look at the positive not the negative. Everyone has a story, many worse than yours.

Approach every situation as a challenge, not a frustration.

Be flexible. Don't be afraid to change direction.

Recognize opportunity when it strikes.

Don't be afraid to make mistakes. I found it to be the best learning tool.

Have a passion for what you do.

Know yourself, know your strengths and capitalize on them.

Whatever you get into, make sure you have a safe way out.